MY HEALTHY HABITS

TEETH CARE
FOR A BRIGHT SMILE

NorwoodHouse Press

Madison Parker

Cataloging-in-Publication Data

Names: Parker, Madison.
Title: Teeth care for a bright smile / Madison Parker.
Description: Buffalo, NY : Norwood House Press, 2026. | Series: My healthy habits | Includes glossary and index.
Identifiers: ISBN 9781978575462 (pbk.) | ISBN 9781978575479 (library bound) | ISBN 9781978575486 (ebook)
Subjects: LCSH: Teeth--Care and hygiene--Juvenile literature.
Classification: LCC RK63.P375 2026 | DDC 617.5'22--dc23

Published in 2026 by
Norwood House Press
2544 Clinton Street
Buffalo, NY 14224

Copyright © 2026 Norwood House Press
Designer: Rhea Magaro
Editor: Kim Thompson

Photo credits: Cover, p. 1 Odua Images/Shutterstock.com; p. 5 Studio Romantic/Shutterstock.com; p. 6 Mercury Green/Shutterstock.com; p. 7 baibaz/Shutterstock.com; p. 8 Peter Hermes Furian/Shutterstock.com; p. 9 New Africa/Shutterstock.com; p. 10 WBMUL/Shutterstock.com; p. 11 Mehmet Cetin/Shutterstock.com; p. 12 BIGANDT.COM/Shutterstock.com; p. 14 Olga Popova/Shutterstock.com; p. 15 Alexandra Morosanu/Shutterstock.com; pp. 17, 18 Drazen Zigic/Shutterstock.com; p. 19 PeopleImages.comYuri A/Shutterstock.com; p. 21 ESB Professional/Shutterstock.com;

Printed in the United States of America

Some of the images in this book illustrate individuals who are models. The depictions do not imply actual situations or events.

CPSIA compliance information: Batch #CSNHP26: For further information contact Norwood House Press at 1-800-237-9932.

Find us on

TABLE OF CONTENTS

CARING FOR YOUR TEETH IS IMPORTANT

It is important to keep your teeth healthy. Practicing good habits every day will make your teeth strong and your smile bright!

HEALTHY FOODS FOR YOUR TEETH

Crunchy fruits and veggies help clean your teeth as you chew. They also provide **vitamins** that your body uses to keep your teeth healthy. Foods like apples and carrots are good choices.

Milk, cheese, and yogurt are full of **calcium**. Your body uses calcium to build strong bones and teeth.

Sugary snacks like candy and soda can hurt your teeth. They weaken the hard **enamel** that covers your teeth. Nuts, fruits, and other healthy snacks are better for your teeth.

Water is the best drink for keeping your teeth healthy. Water washes away food and keeps your mouth clean.

BRUSHING YOUR TEETH

Brushing your teeth gets rid of food and **germs**. Brushing keeps your teeth clean and your breath fresh.

Use toothpaste with **fluoride** to make your teeth stronger. Fluoride helps protect your teeth from **cavities**.

Brush your teeth for two minutes twice a day. Be sure to gently brush all sides of your teeth, even in the back.

FLOSSING YOUR TEETH

Flossing cleans between your teeth where a toothbrush can't reach. It removes tiny bits of food that can cause cavities.

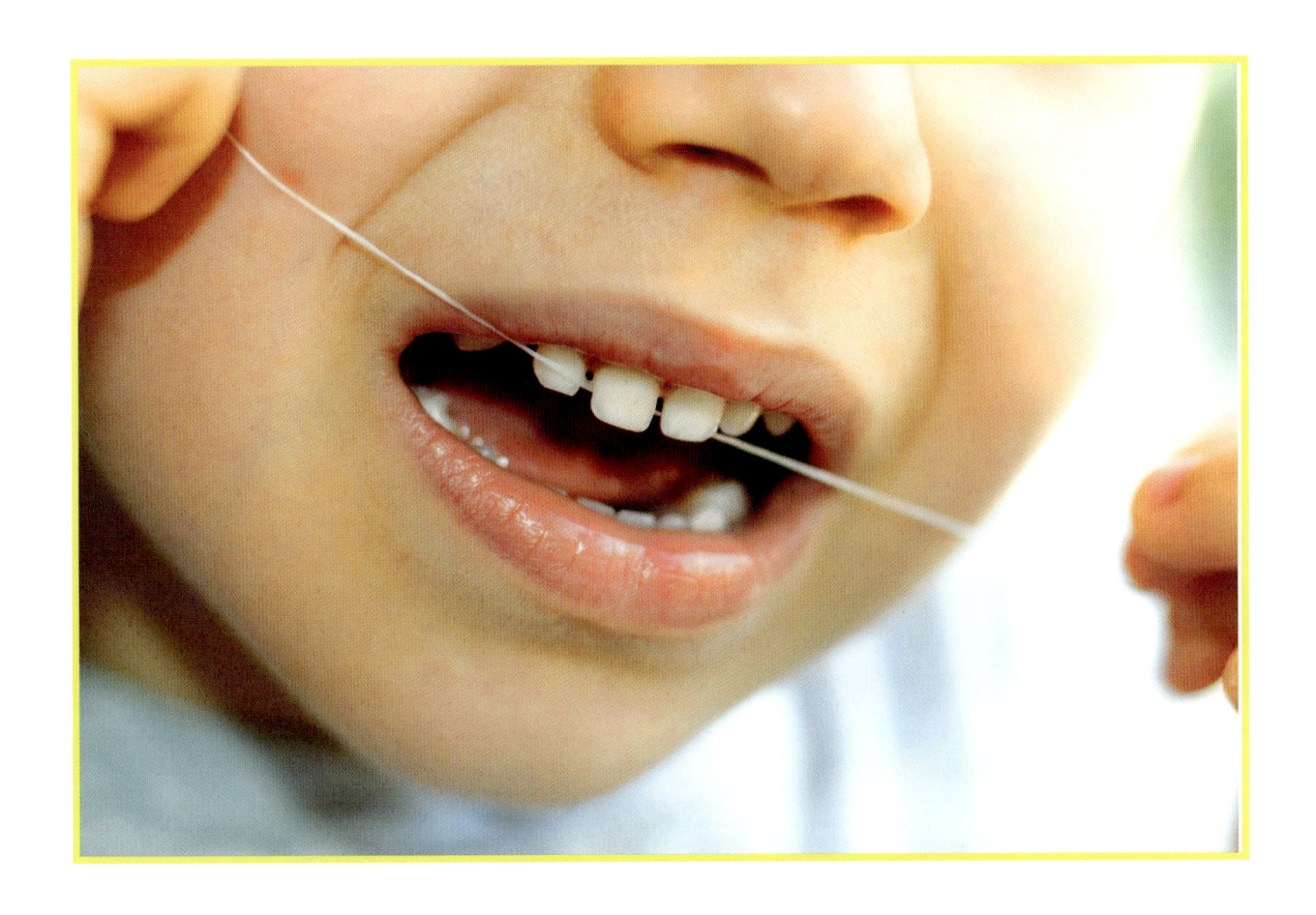

You should floss once each day. Slide the floss gently between your teeth. Be careful not to hurt your **gums**.

GOING TO THE DENTIST

Dentists are doctors who care for teeth. They check your teeth to make sure they are strong and healthy. It's important to visit the dentist twice a year for a checkup.

At the dentist's office, a **dental hygienist** gives your teeth a special cleaning to remove **plaque**. The hygienist might also give you tips for taking care of your teeth at home.

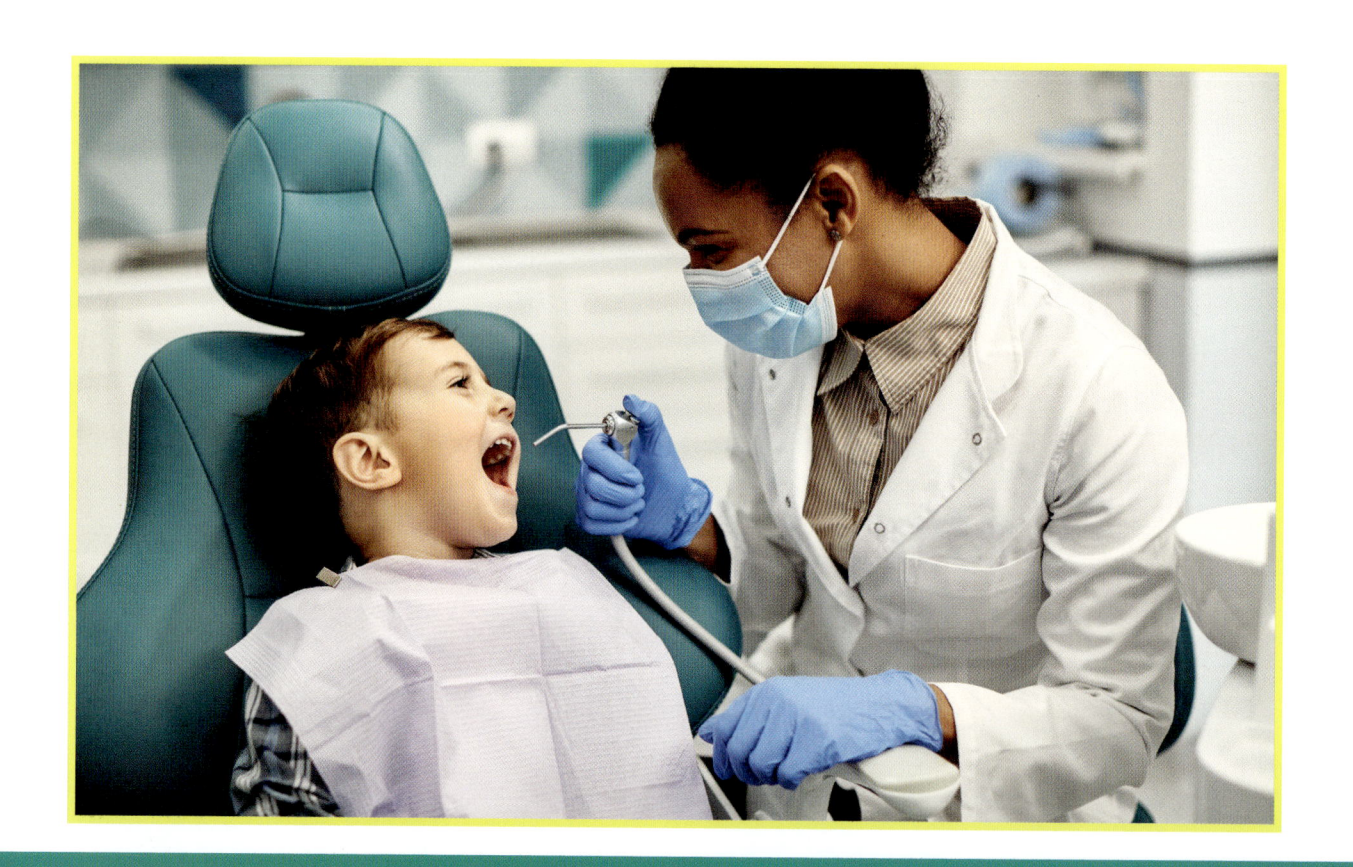

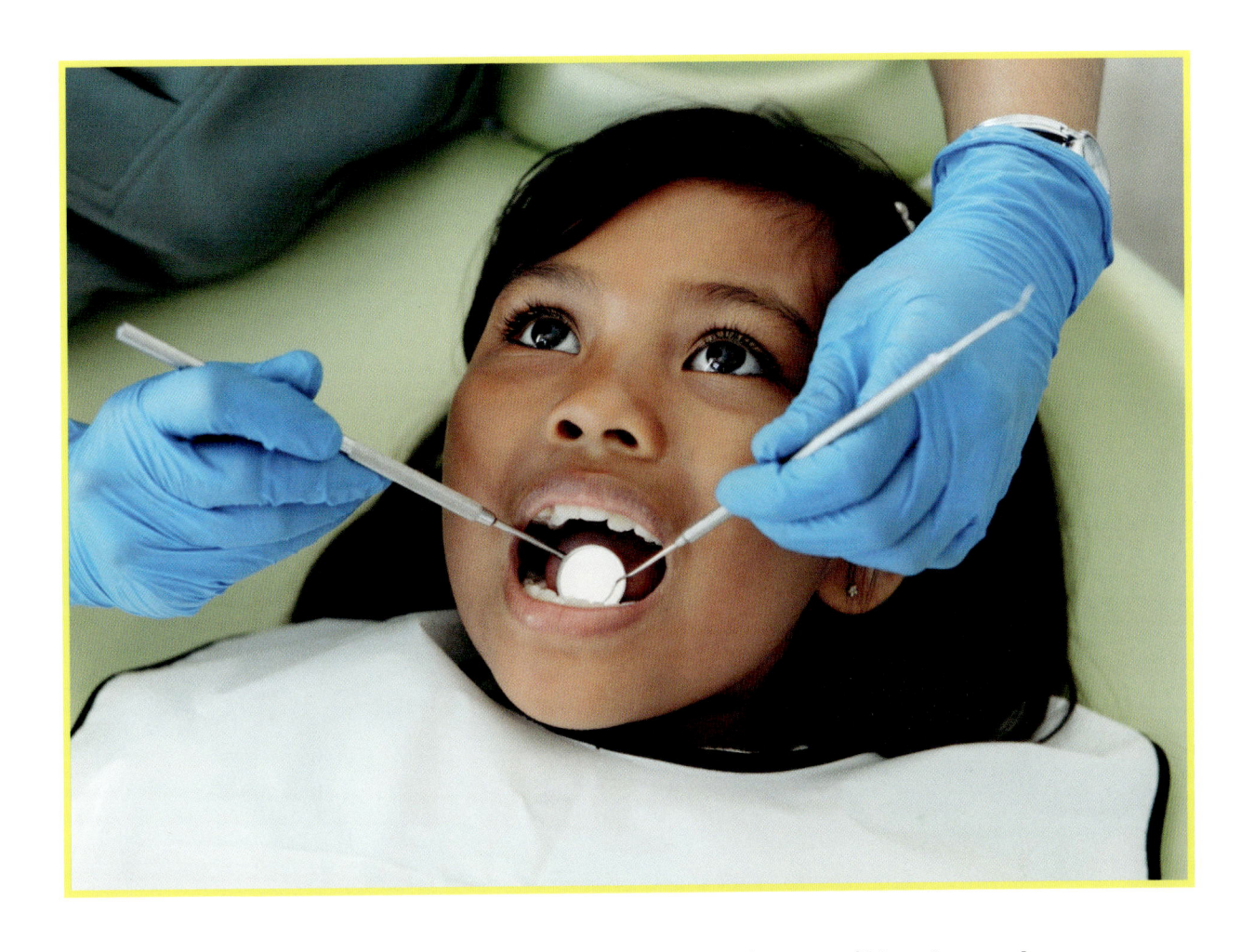

After your cleaning, the dentist will check your teeth and gums. If anything needs fixing, the dentist can help right away.

WHITE, BRIGHT, AND HEALTHY

Taking care of your teeth is important. It is easy, too! Eat healthy foods, brush, floss, and visit the dentist to keep your smile bright!

GLOSSARY

calcium (KAL-see-uhm): a mineral that is found in dairy foods and that is needed for strong teeth and bones

cavities (KAV-i-teez): holes in the teeth caused by decay

dental hygienist (DEN-tuhl hye-JEE-nist): a person trained to help keep people's teeth clean and healthy

enamel (i-NAM-uhl): the hard, white surface of your teeth

flossing (FLAH-sing): using a special string to clean between teeth and remove food and plaque

fluoride (FLOR-ide): a mineral in toothpaste and water that helps protect teeth from getting cavities

germs (jurmz): tiny living things that can make you sick or cause cavities

gums (guhmz): areas of firm, pink skin around the roots of your teeth

plaque (plak): a sticky layer of germs that can build up on teeth and cause cavities

vitamins (VYE-tuh-minz): important parts of food that help your body and teeth stay strong and healthy

THINKING QUESTIONS

1. How many times should you brush your teeth each day?

2. How does flossing help keep your teeth clean?

3. What foods are good for your teeth? Why?

4. How does fluoride in toothpaste protect your teeth from cavities?

5. Why is it important to visit the dentist regularly for checkups?

INDEX

ABOUT THE AUTHOR

Madison Parker spent her childhood in the city of Chicago, Illinois. A farm girl at heart, today she lives in Wisconsin with her husband and four children on a small farm with cows, goats, chickens, and two miniature horses named Harley and David. Her favorite dessert is vanilla frozen custard with rainbow sprinkles, even in the winter.